John Ward

Motifs for panels and other decoration

John Ward

Motifs for panels and other decoration

ISBN/EAN: 9783337413873

Printed in Europe, USA, Canada, Australia, Japan

Cover: Foto ©Andreas Hilbeck / pixelio.de

More available books at **www.hansebooks.com**

MOTIFS

FOR PANEL AND OTHER DECORATION

BY · JOHN · WARD · BIRMINGHAM

1881.

INTRODUCTION.

————:o:————

IN producing the following Work, it has been my aim to give a series of suggestions that will readily lend themselves to the various processes of Art Manufacture. I have frequently felt the want of such suggestions, when there has not been the necessary time or inclination to obtain the details for such purposes. Many of my friends have also expressed their experience of the same deficiency. It is with the object of meeting this requirement that the present Work has been undertaken.

THE details have been carefully thought out, and drawn in a manner I think best suited for the purpose for which they are intended, and treated so that they may readily suggest themselves as motifs to whomsoever may turn to these pages. In compiling the plates, the necessity of making them as general as possible in character has been kept in view, in order that they may be of equal service to the Designer, Decorative Artist, Cabinet-Maker, Earthenware Manufacturer, Japanner, Metal Worker, and, in fact, to every branch of Art Industry. Knowing practically the requirements and taste of the present period, I have adopted what appears to be the best method of drawing, in the various popular styles, so that, with comparatively small artistic knowledge, the designs may be adapted to all processes.

IN addition to the utility of this Work to the Manufacturing world, I hope it may prove of great service to Amateurs who devote their leisure hours to painting on China, Fabrics, &c., as they will find it valuable, not only for the motifs it contains, but as a means of teaching them, by a little careful study, to compose similar examples out of odd bits of nature they may wish to adopt. It will further enable them to distinguish the method of treatment natural objects require to ensure the necessary boldness and vigour which cannot be obtained if nature be copied too servilely.

This Work being simply one of illustration, I have made the preface as brief as possible, and, in conclusion, thank those friends who have already promised me their assistance and patronage.

J. W.

Birmingham, April, 1881.

PLATE. I.

Photo-lith. P. L. Monteney Natta

Photo Lithographed and Printed by P.T.Mountenay. N.9 ?!

PLATE. III.

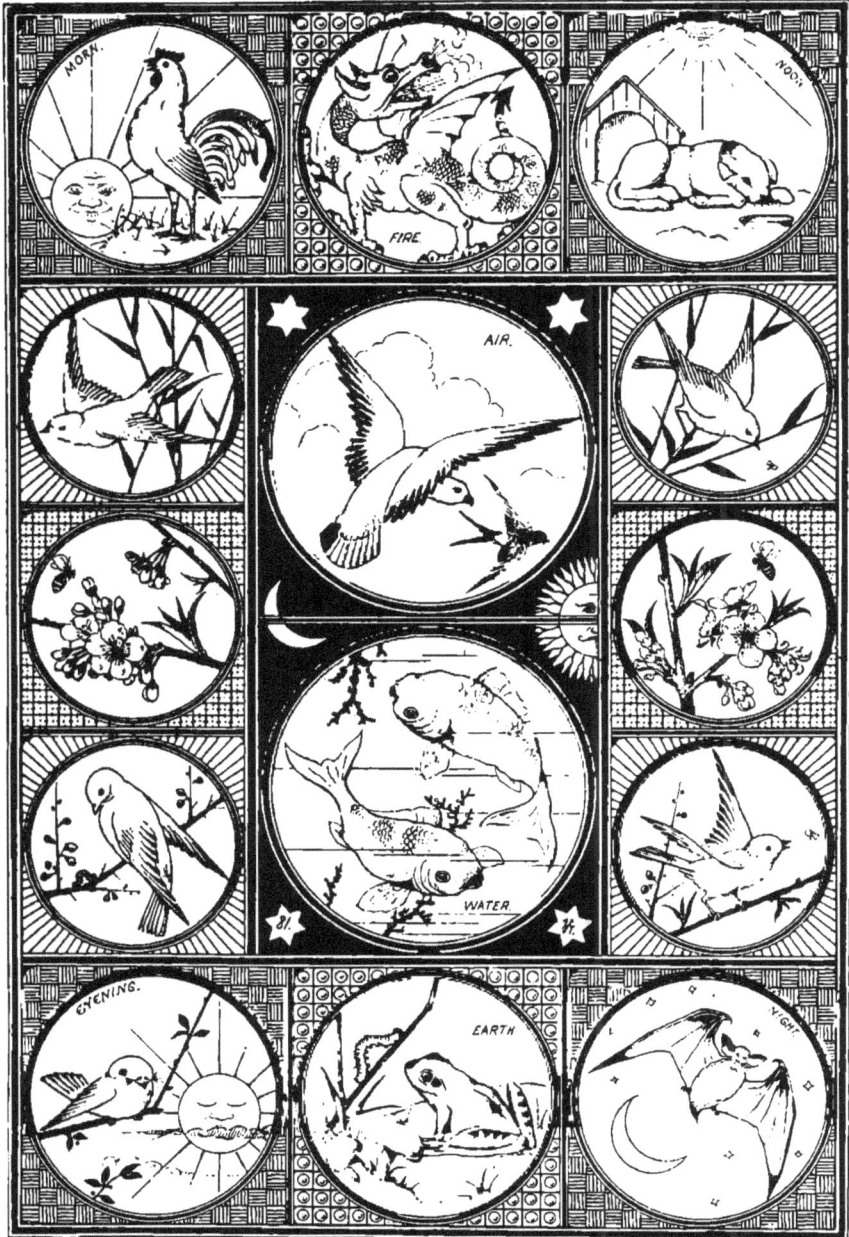

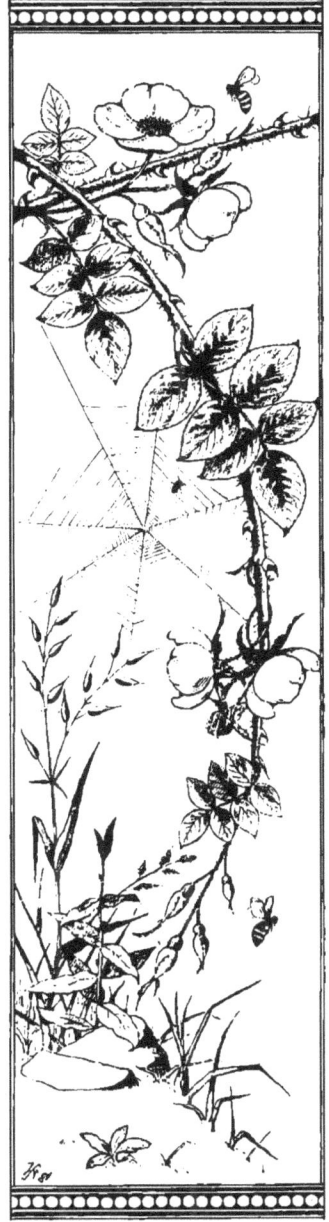

PLATE. IV.

PLATE. V.

Photo Lithographed and Printed by H.T.Mountenay, Nott.ᵐ

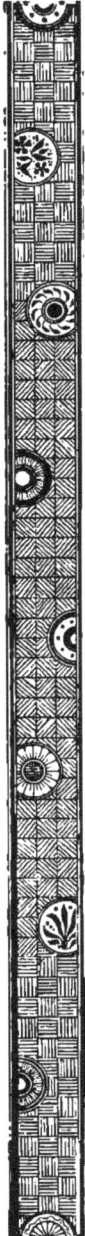

PLATE VI.

PLATE VII.

PLATE VII

STAG DRINKING

THE CROW AND THE PITCHER

STAG DRINKING

THE FOX AND

THE STORK (2)

THE FOX & GRAPES

THE FOX & THE RAVEN

THE DOG AND HIS SHADOW

THE HARE AND THE TORTOISE

KING SUN SUNG LOG

PLATE IX.

PLATE X

Plate X.

PLATE XI

PLATE XII.

PLATE. XIII.

PLATE XIV.

APPLE BLOSSOM.

PASSION FLOWER.

BLACKBERRY.

IVY.

ROSE.

PLATE XV

PLATE XVI

PLATE XVII

Photo Litho P. J. Mountain. &c.

PLATE XVIII.

RAW MATERIAL.

Pub. John P.T. Montross, N.Y.Co.

PLATE. XIX.

PLATE XX.

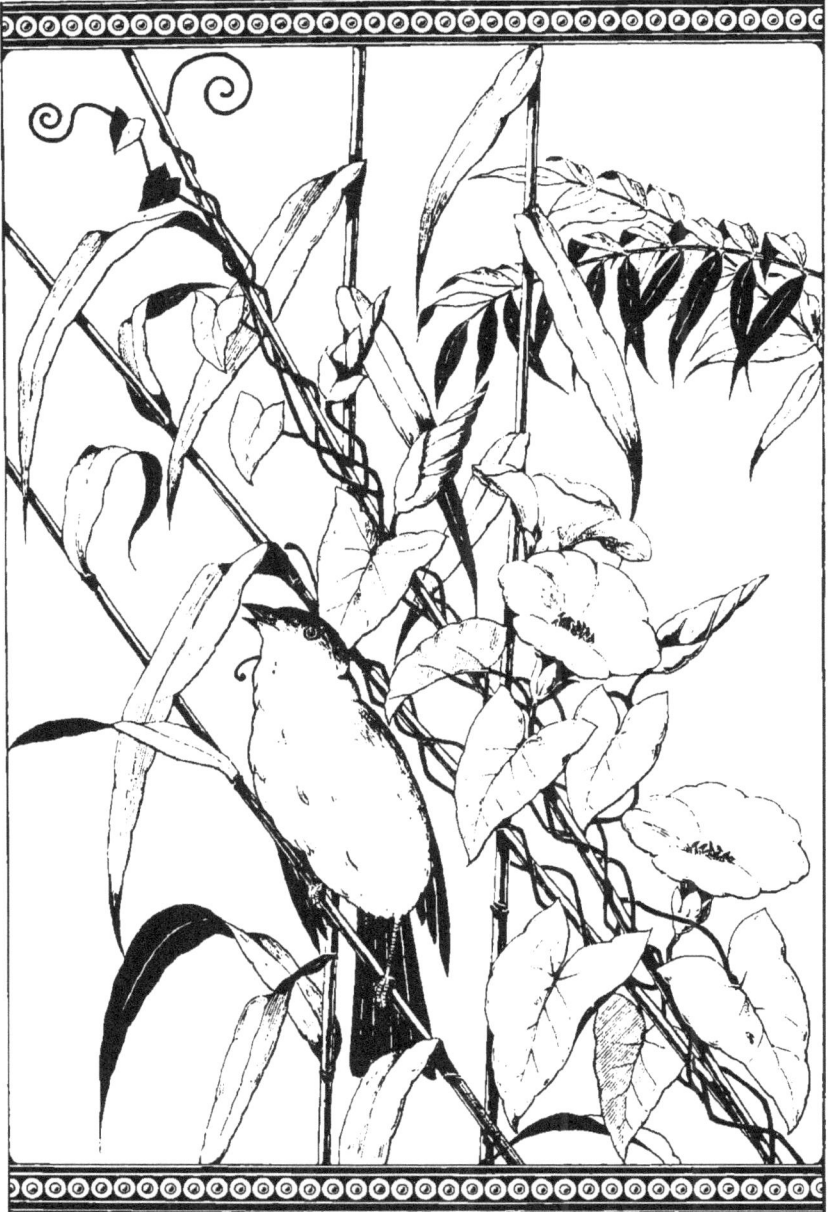

www.ingramcontent.com/pod-product-compliance
Lightning Source LLC
Chambersburg PA
CBHW021600270326
41931CB00009B/1319